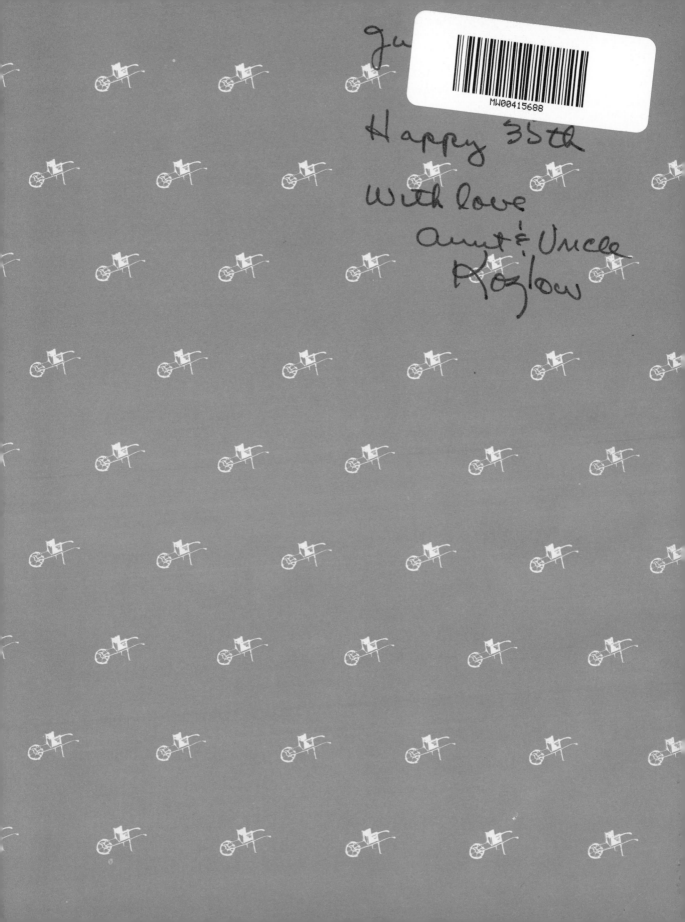

gu

Happy 35th

With love
aunt & Uncle
Kozlow

A GARDEN TREASURY

A WATERMARK PRESS BOOK

First published in Great Britian by
Simon & Schuster Limited 1987
© 1987 The Watermark Press

This book is copyright under the Berne Convention.
No reproduction without permission.
All rights reserved.
Simon & Schuster Limited, West Garden Place,
Kendal Street, London W2 2AQ

British Library Cataloguing in Publication Data
Blackall, Elizabeth
A garden treasury.
1. English literature. 2. Gardens –
Literary collections
I. Title
820.2'036   PR1111.G3
ISBN 0-671-65517-5

Typeset in Australia by Keyset Phototype
Printed and Bound in Singapore by
Imago Productions (F.E.) Pte. Ltd.

A
GARDEN
TREASURY

*A celebration of gardens
and gardeners
in poetry and prose*

—— *compiled by* ——

ELIZABETH BLACKALL

SIMON SCHUSTER

TRANSPLANTING AND TAKING CUTTINGS –
FROM 'THE GARDENER'S
LABYRINTH 1651'. THOMAS HYLL.
'AT WHAT TIMES DIVERS PLANTS SPRUNG UP, OUGHT TO BE REMOVED AND SET
AGAIN, AS OUT OF ONE BED OR BORDER INTO ANOTHER, WITH THE BREAKING
OR SLIPPING OF SUNDRY SETS FROM OLD BODIES, WHICH WITH SKIL REQUIRES
TO BE BESTOWED IN THE EARTH . . .

A garden is a lovesome thing, God wot!
Rose plot, Fringed pool, Ferned grot
The veriest school
Of peace; and yet the fool
Contends that God is not
Not God! in gardens! when the eve is cool?
Nay, but I have a sign:
'Tis very sure God walks in mine.

T E Brown – My Garden

Contents

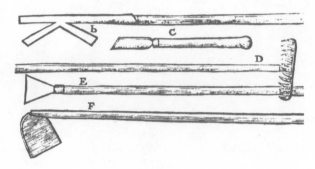

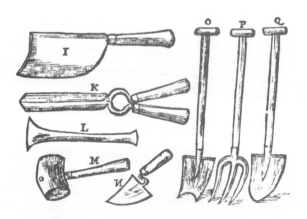

'DELICIOUS WEATHER'

AN ETCHING BY JAMES GILLRAY 1808, SHOWING AN INGENIOUS GARDEN

SEAT.

IN THE BEGINNING

The word Eden means delight, Eden means Paradise, Eden was a garden, lost in antiquity.

We know there were walled gardens in Egypt three thousand years ago, with a system of irrigation and possibly a pool with fish. Vines were trained on the walls so that there would be cool shade. This was the style of the first gardens of the world, the style which continued and developed in Persia, the Islamic countries and Greece for thousands of years.

Time passed; in the gardens fruit trees were planted, then flowers. In Persian miniature paintings and in the designs of their carpets can be seen lilies, poppies, narcissi and roses; in Homer's 'Odyssey' we read of the large walled garden of Alcinous. Today, perfectly maintained, with little cascades of water flowing through the terraces, we can see the gardens of the Generalife, a legacy of the Moors, in Granada.

The Romans introduced the courtyard as part of the house, bright with flowers. Their growing interest in horticulture found expression in the gardens of their country villas, where with a few acres they grew salads, root vegetables, asparagus, parsley, as well as fruit trees. During the Roman occupation of Britain they continued to cultivate their vineyards as well as their gardens.

After the Romans left Britain, their arts were forgotten and gradually the gardens disappeared through neglect. However it is interesting to know that some of their plants naturalised, and, among the weeds, leeks, beans and even cabbages struggled for existence.

It was not until some centuries later that the garden reappeared in the cloisters of monasteries and cathedrals.

Our knowledge of the gardens made in the distant past is limited, but it is clear that the garden was primarily a private place to take the air, confined by walls and possibly paved, with plants of secondary though functional importance.

It was in a later age that man saw a garden as something more, a place intended, designed for plants in all their beauty and usefulness.

It was some time before gardening in England reached the level of that in Europe, but with the establishment of the monasteries and the coming of the Normans, interest and skills were revived, and in castle and cloister the small garden developed, rectangular and neat, with small beds or knots sometimes little more than six feet square, set in an intricate pattern marked by a miniature hedge. The spaces left by this pattern were usually filled with herbs, although where the knot garden was purely decorative, instead of plants one might see sand or coloured stones. Herbs were probably the first plants of the English garden, together with vegetables, and then small flowers, pansies, pinks, wallflowers and numerous others that have remained with us through the centuries.

The medieval gardeners are nameless; no medieval gardens now exist in England, though in many places such gardens have been recreated on their original site.

Within the scope of a small book one cannot give a history of gardening, but some idea of the development of this delightful English art can be traced through a long line of imaginative and skilful gardeners.

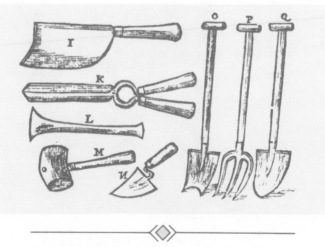

A 1649 ILLUSTRATION OF A GARDENER'S ARMORY, WITH POSSIBLY THE
EARLIEST DEPICTION OF A TRIANGULAR TROWEL AND A DIGGING FORK.

Three
Centuries Of
Gardens
And Gardeners

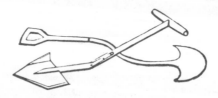

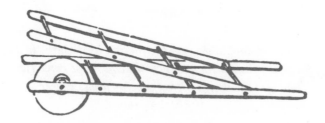

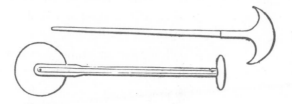

Herein were the olde husbandes very careful and used always to judge that where they found the Garden out of order, the wife of the house (for unto her belonged the charge thereof) was no good huswyfe.

BARNABY GOOGE 1390

SIR THOMAS MORE (1478-1535)

After the fall of Wolsey, More was consulted by Henry VIII for his ideas on gardening. In 1520 he bought land by the River Thames in what was then the village of Chelsea, and established a small farm and farmhouse, set in a beautiful garden with trees, flowers and fruit. Beyond stretched meadows and woodland and a fine view of the river.

Part of his garden was set aside for his servants, that they might work there in their leisure.

No plans remain of this garden, but Miles Hadfield notes, in his 'History of British Gardening', that 'we have in a little painting of More and his family (in the Sotheby Collection) one of the few glimpses by a contemporary of an early sixteenth century garden – though, having been planned by More, it was presumably in advance of its time'. It is possible, says Hadfield, that the rosemary which grows today in many a Chelsea garden was introduced there by Sir Thomas More, who liked 'to let it run over his garden walks, not only because his bees loved it, but because 'tis the herb sacred to remembrance and therefore to friendship'.

Hadfield adds: 'It is not surrounded by those embattled walls which protect the guilty conscience of a Stafford or a Wolsey; the eye looks over a neat geometrical pattern of beds – hedged, we may assume, with rosemary – to the Thames. A wall, against which lie trained fruit trees, runs down one side of the garden; it ends, not in a turret, but a tall garden house. The whole design is one of simplicity. Reason, one feels, underlies its planning. It is far removed from the scenes shown in medieval miniatures, nor has it any hint of Mediterranean drama or French extravagance. It is, indeed, Utopian in its simplicity and sensibilities, and we may guess, one of the first examples of a garden in a tradition that has become typically English'.

A WALL HERBER, FROM 'THE GARDENERS LABYRINTH'.

They set great store by their gardens. In them they have vineyards, all manner of fruit, herbs and flowers, so pleasant, so well furnished, and so finely kept, that I never saw thing more fruitful nor better trimmed in any place. Their study and diligence herein cometh not only of pleasure, but also of certain strife and contention that is between street and street, concerning the trimming husbanding and furnishing of their gardens, every man for his own part. And verily you shall not lightly find in all the city anything that is more commodious, either for the profit of the citizens or for pleasure. And therefore it may seem that the first founder of the city minded nothing so much as he did these gardens.

SIR THOMAS MORE 1518 – FROM THE UTOPIA

FRANCIS BACON (1561-1626) Statesman, essayist.
His essay, 'Of Gardens', much quoted, sets out instructions for the creation of a formal garden on a 30 acre site. This concise account gives a clear picture of how gardens for great houses may have been designed in Stuart times. His own garden at Gorhambury, St. Albans, is described in detail by John Aubrey, and the garden at Theobalds, created by James I, was probably a copy of Gorhambury.

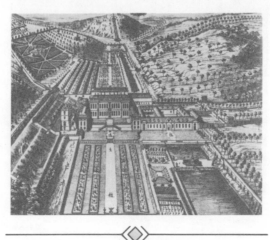

DYRHAM, GLOUCESTERSHIRE,
BEGUN IN 1694 AND NOW A NATIONAL TRUST PROPERTY.

The garden is large, which was (no doubt) rarely planted and kept in His Lordship's time. Here is a handsome Dore, which opens into Oake-wood: . . . The Oakes of this wood are very great and shadie. His Lordship much delighted himselfe here: under every tree, he planted some fine flower, or flowers, some whereof are there still (1656) viz. Paeonies, Tullips.

From this wood a dore opens into a place as big as an ordinary Barke, the west part whereof is Coppice-wood, where are Walkes cut out as straight as a line and broad enough for a Coach, a quarter of a mile long or better. Here His Lordship much meditated, his servant Mr Bushell attending him with his pen and inke home to sett downe his present Notions.

The east of this Parquet was heretofore, in his Lordship's prosperitie, a Paradise; now is a large ploughed field. The walkes, both in the coppices and other Boscages, were most ingeniousely designed; at severall good Viewes, were erected elegant Sommer-howses well-built of Roman architecture, well wainscotted and cieled; yet standing, but defaced, so that one would have thought the Barbarians had made a Conquest here.

The figures of the Ponds were thus: they were pitched at the bottomes with pebbles of severall colours, which were work't in to several figures, as of Fishes etc., which in His Lordship's time were plainly to be seen through the cleare water, now overgrown with flagges and rushes. If a poore bodie had brought His Lordship half a dozen pebbles of a curious colour, he would give them a shilling, so curious was he in perfecting his Fish-ponds, which I guesse doe containe four acres. In the middle of the middlemost pond, in the Island, is a curious banquetting house of Roman architecture, paved with black and white marble; covered with Cornish slatt, and neatly wainscotted.

JOHN AUBREY (1625-1697), WRITING ABOUT FRANCIS BACON'S GARDEN AT GORHAMBURY (VERULAM).

The pleasure and Use of Gardens were unknown to our great Grandfathers: They were contented with Pot-herbs: and did mind chiefly their Stables. But in the time of King Charles II Gardening was much improved, and became common. 'Twas Sir John Danvers of Chelsey (Brother and Heir to Henry Danvers Earle of Danby) who first taught us the way of Italian gardens: He had well travelled France and Italy, and made good Observations: He had a very fine Fancy, which lay (chiefly) for Gardens, and Architecture. The Garden at Chelsey in Middlesex (as likewise the House there) doe remaine Monuments of his Ingenuity. He was a great acquaintance and Favorite of the Lord Chancellor Bacon, who took much delight in that elegant Garden.

JOHN AUBREY WRITING ABOUT SIR JOHN DANVERS (1588-1655)

JOHN TRADESCANT (1580 – 1638)

Considered by many to be the first of the great English gardeners, Tradescant was Head Gardener at Hatfield before entering the service first of Lord Wotton at Canterbury, and later of the Duke of Buckingham. While at Hatfield he was commissioned by Robert Cecil to collect plants in Europe. From Holland he purchased roses, shrubs, cherry trees and mulberries, bulbs and irises. He bought anemones, probably unknown in England at that time. Finally he was appointed as Head Gardener to Charles I.

At Hatfield House, on the main staircase one of the newel posts has a carving of a gardener dressed in early 17th century fashion, with a rake and a basket laden with fruit. It is believed to be a portrait of John Tradescant.

There is no ancient gentlemen but gardeners.

SHAKESPEARE – HAMLET

JOHN PARKINSON (1567 – 1650)

Botanist, apothecary and writer, is best remembered for his 'Paradise in Sole Paradisus Terrestris — *A garden of all sorts of pleasant flowers which our English ayre will permitt to be noursed up: with a kitchen garden of all manner of herbes, rootes and fruites, for meat or sauce used with us, and an orchard of all sorte of fruitbearing Trees and Shrubbes fit for our Land together with the right ordering planting and preserving of them and their uses and vertues.* Collected by John Parkinson Apothecary of London 1629'.

This delightful book reveals the author's sensitive love of plants and his careful observation. He lists nearly a thousand plants and has provided some eight hundred meticulous illustrations.

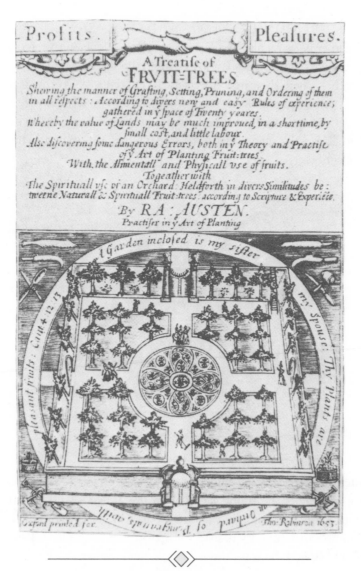

RALPH AUSTEN'S 'A TREATISE OF FRUIT TREES' 1653 EXPOUNDED HIS
ECCENTRIC THEORY THAT GROWING FRUIT WOULD SOLVE THE
COUNTRY'S PROBLEMS.

JOHN TRADESCANT II (1608 – 1662)

Like his father he was a plant collector, travelling widely in search of rare and attractive plants. The Tradescants had their own botanic gardens – The Ark at Lambeth – where their new discoveries were tended. On the death of his father the young John took his place in the Royal Household, and remained there until the execution of Charles I, when he returned to his home and garden in Lambeth, spending the rest of his life working with his famous plant collection.

UNUSUAL FOR THE MIDDLE AGES, A THREE-WHEELED WHEELBARROW.

ANDRE LE NOTRE (1613 – 1700)

In his lifetime he had considerable influence upon English garden-designers. Le Notre was one of the young gardeners at the Tuileries who later designed the famous gardens at Vaux le Vicomte. Louis XIV greatly admired his work and commissioned him to design the gardens at Versailles. Despite the grandeur of his work he was an unassuming man. When the King suggested that he might like to have a coat of arms, Le Notre jokingly replied that the only suitable one would be a spade with three slugs and a decoration of cabbage leaves. In the early 18th century his influence was seen in the new fashion for landscape gardening.

Large or small, the garden should look both orderly and rich. It should be well fenced from the outher world. It should by no means imitate either the wilfulness or the wildness of Nature, but should look like a thing never seen except near a house.

WILLIAM MORRIS — HOPES & FEARS FOR ART.

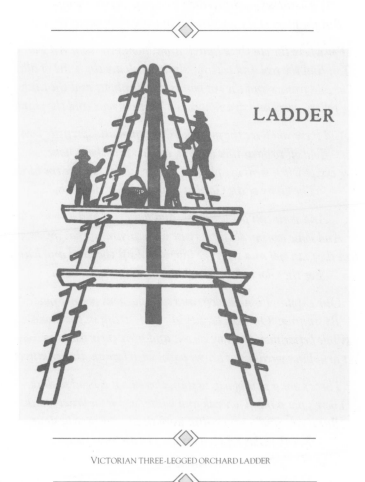

LADDER

VICTORIAN THREE-LEGGED ORCHARD LADDER

The Glory of the Garden

Our England is a garden that is full of stately views,
Of borders beds and shrubberies, and lawns and avenues,
With statues on the terraces and peacocks strutting by;
But the glory of the garden lies in more than meets the eye.

For where the old thick laurels grow, along the thin red wall
You find the tool and potting-sheds which are the heart of all;
The cold frames and the hot houses, the dungpits and the tanks,
The rollers, carts and drainpipes, with the barrows and the planks.

And there you'll see the gardeners, the men and 'prentice boys
Told off to do as they are bid, and do it without noise;
For except when seeds are planted and we shout to scare the birds.
The Glory of the Garden it abideth not in words.

And some can pot begonias, and some can bud a rose,
And some are hardly fit to trust with anything that grows;
But they can roll and trim the lawns and sift the sand and loam,
For the Glory of the Garden occupieth all who come.

Our England is a garden, and such gardens are not made
By singing: 'Oh, how beautiful', and sitting in the shade,
While better men than we go out and start their working lives
At grubbing weeds from gravel paths with broken dinner knives.

There's not a pair of legs so thin, there's not a head so thick,
There's not a hand so weak and white, nor yet a heart so sick,
But it can find some needful work that's crying to be done,
For the Glory of the Garden glorifieth everyone.

Then seek your job with thankfulness and work till further orders,
If it's only netting strawberries or killing slugs on borders;
And when your back stops aching and your hands begin to harden,
You will find yourself a partner in the Glory of the Garden.

Oh, Adam was a gardener, and God who made him sees
That half a proper gardener's work is done upon his knees,
So when your work is finished, you can wash your hands and pray
For the Glory of the Garden, that it may not pass away!
And the Glory of the Garden it shall never pass away!

RUDYARD KIPLING – THE GLORY OF THE GARDEN

A HAND SIEVE OF 1630.

A SQUARE SIEVE OF 1706, USED ESPECIALLY FOR REMOVING STONES.

JOHN EVELYN (1620 – 1706)

He is remembered chiefly for his Diary, his 'Kalendarium Hortense: *the Gardener's Almanack, Directing what he is to do monthly throughout the year, and what fruits and flowers are in prime*'. All gardeners would agree with him that 'A Gardener's Work is never at an end; it begins with the Year, and continues to the next'. His book 'Sylva, a Discourse of Forest Trees', written in 1664, encouraged schemes of tree planting and brought a lasting interest in the cultivation of a wide variety of trees throughout the country.

19TH CENTURY VERGE AND GRASS SHEARS.

SIR WILLIAM TEMPLE (1628 – 1699)

He was a scholar, politician and writer as well as an imaginative garden designer. In his book 'Gardening in the year 1685' he described his garden at Moor Park which expressed his ideas on the beauty of irregularity.

'In every garden four things are necessary to be provided for, Flowers, Fruit, Shade and Water, and whoever lays out a garden without all these must not pretend it in any perfection. It ought to lie to the best parts of the House, or to those of the Master's commonest use, so as to be but like one of the rooms out of which you step into another.'

There are a few magnificent old gardening books written by learned scholars, but I think the majority of us love most those written by homely folk, who not only owned gardens, but worked therein themselves, for their books are redolent of the soil and of lifelong intimate friendship with plants. Hyll emphasises that he himself was not a man of much learning. In his preface he speaks of his 'rudeness of pen', and says that never having 'tasted of the learned laake but rather always rudely taught' his book is for 'the simple and unlettered'.

He goes on to say 'Seeing Therefore . . . that I shall not obtain the frendlye countenaunce of all men yet I do not doubt, but the wyse wyl geve me their good worde and will cosider myne intent, as it is indede: that is to please the common sort, for whose onelye sake, I have taken these paines and have published this Booke'. Then Hyll leads one into the small garden depicted on the title page of his book.

ELEANOUR SINCLAIR ROHDE – *THE OLD ENGLISH GARDENING BOOKS*

GEORGE LONDON and HENRY WISE (1653-1738)

Nurserymen and gardeners, they were partners in the flourishing, internationally-known Brompton Nurseries. Together they made translations of French works on gardening. They laid out gardens at Hampton Court and at Wanstead. The latter was described by Daniel Defoe in 1714 as the finest garden in the world.

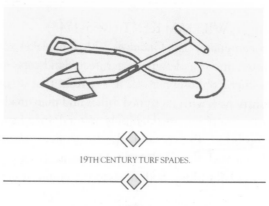

19TH CENTURY TURF SPADES.

JOSEPH ADDISON (1672-1719)

This essayist – like Sir William Temple and the poet Alexander Pope – had wearied of formality in the garden. Addison, writing in the *Spectator:* 'British Gardeners, instead of humouring Nature, love to deviate from it as much as possible. Our trees rise in Cones, Globes and Pyramids. We see the marks of scissors upon every Plant and Bush. I do not know whether I am singular in my opinion, but, for my own part, I would rather look upon a tree in all its Luxuriancy and Diffusion of Boughs and Branches, than when it is thus cut and trimmed into a Mathematical Figure, and cannot but fancy that an Orchard in Flower looks infinitely more delightful than all the little Labyrinths of the most finished Parterre'.

Writing in the *Spectator* about Kitchen Gardens, he observes: ' I have always thought a kitchen garden a more pleasant sight than the finest orangery . . . I love to see everything in perfection, and am more pleased to survey my rows of coleworts and cabbages, with a thousand nameless pot herbs springing up in their full fragrancy and verdure, than to see the tender plants of foreign countries.'

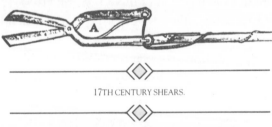

17TH CENTURY SHEARS.

WILLIAM KENT (1685-1748)

Recording his tricentenary, *The Guardian* 20th June 1984 writes: 'William Kent was a painter, interior designer, architect, landscape gardener, book illustrator and aesthetic philosopher . . . It is to Kent that we owe the look of the English Country park with its ruined follies and man-made lakes, highly artificial in construction but maddeningly natural in effect. Kent is the precursor of Capability Brown and the first great champion of the picturesque.' He created the gardens at Stowe in Buckinghamshire and Rousham House in Oxfordshire, both open to the public at certain times.

BOUGAINVILLEA CASCADES OVER THE WINDOW OF A HOUSE IN SYDNEY,
AUSTRALIA

CHATEAU VILLANDRY, NEAR TOURS,
SHOWING PART OF THE FAMOUS
PARTERRE

ALEXANDER POPE (1688-1744)

Poet, philospher and gardener, Pope created a charming small garden at Twickenham greatly admired in his day. A critic of the formal gardens of the earlier designers, in an article in *The Guardian* he advocated a freer, less formal style. In 1744 Walpole described his Twickenham garden as 'a singular effort of art and taste to impress so much variety and scenery on a spot of five acres.'

With Pope and his followers, gardeners looked beyond the confines of walls and terraces and began to see the English Countryside as a setting which would enhance the beauty of the English garden.

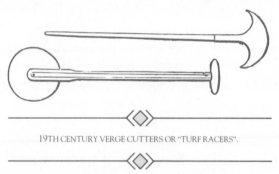

19TH CENTURY VERGE CUTTERS OR "TURF RACERS".

'CAPABILITY' BROWN (Lancelot Brown 1716-83)

Probably the most famous English landscape gardener, 'Capability' Brown studied with William Kent at Stowe. His naturalistic style can be seen at Blenheim, Chatsworth and Longleat, among other great English country houses. At the time, Brown's rejection of the formal for the naturalistic earned him considerable criticism, but he is now recognized for the genius of his vision. His designs virtually eradicated the formal garden, an intrinsic part of the English gardening heritage. In its place was an expanse of grass, covering the estate and surrounding the house. His contemporaries, bitter about the destruction of the English tradition by Brown and his imitators, complained of the monotony of his landscapes, 'one uniform, eternal green'.

'Capability' Brown's enormous contribution to landscaping has now been widely acknowledged, and his conception of parkland design seen as natural and right.

HUMPHREY REPTON (1752-1818)

Was considered to have succeeded 'Capability' Brown as England's leading landscape gardener, though later he questioned Brown's ideas for landscapes with their smooth bald surfaces. Writing in 1797, Repton said:

'Why this art has been called 'landscape gardening' perhaps he who gave it the title may explain. I can see no reason, unless it be the efficacy which it has shown in destroying landscapes, in which, indeed, it seems infallible . . . .'

It was Repton who brought flowers back to the English garden; gardens were related to the architecture of the house, and once more there were terraces and avenues. Explaining his approach he wrote:

'The perfection of Landscape Gardening consists in the four following requisites: First it must display the natural beauties and hide the natural defects of every situation. Secondly it should give the appearance of extent and freedom, by carefully disguising or hiding the boundary. Thirdly it must studiously conceal every interference of art, however expensive, by which the Scenery is improved, making the whole appear the production of Nature only; and fourthly all objects of mere convenience or comfort, if incapable of being made ornamental, or of becoming parts of the natural scenery, must be removed or concealed.'

Following the reaction from the false landscape school of 'Capability' Brown, the trend moved steadily towards the characteristic English garden of the Elizabethan age.

An authority wrote in 1839:

'Landscape gardening has encroached too much upon gardening proper, and this has had the same effect upon our gardens that horticultural societies have had upon our fruits – to make us entertain the vulgar notion that size is virtue. If I am to have a system at all, give me the good old system of terraces and angled walks, and clipt yew hedges, against whose dark and rich verdure the bright old fashioned flowers glittered in the sun.'

JOHN CLAUDIUS LOUDON (1783-1843)

He was perhaps one of the first writers concerned with the average man who planned a garden and tended it himself. In his preface to the first volume of 'The Gardener's Magazine' he explained that his aim was 'to disseminate new and important information on all topics connected with horticulture and to raise the intellect and the character of those engaged in this art'.

His 'Encyclopaedia of Gardening', published in 1822 was a work of considerable importance.

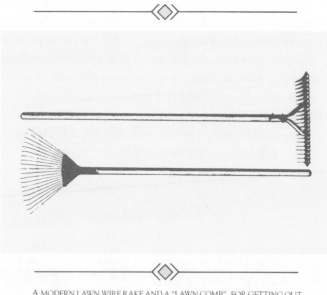

A MODERN LAWN WIRE RAKE AND A "LAWN COMB", FOR GETTING OUT
MOSS AND DEBRIS.

Her heart and interest were not in the large estates with sweeping parklands, but in the small domestic gardens of England which lie within the reach of so many garden lovers. She naturally liked doing big gardens — they paid better, and she was always hard up . . . but it was to the struggling small gardener she appealed.

F. JEKYLL — GERTRUDE JEKYLL, A MEMOIR

As the gardener, so the garden.
THOMAS FULLER – GNOMOLOGIA

Some of the most delightful of all gardens are the little strips in front of roadside cottages. They have a simple and tender charm that one may look for in vain in gardens of greater pretension. And the old garden flowers seem to know that they are seen at their best; for where else can one see such wallflowers or double daisies, or white rose bushes; such clustering masses of perennial peas, or such well-kept flowery edgings of pink or Thrift or London Pride.'
I think that a garden should never be large enough to be tiring, so that if a large space has to be dealt with, a greater part had better be laid out in a wood . . . I do not envy the owners of very large gardens.
GERTRUDE JEKYLL — ON GARDENING

WALL PAINTINGS AT POMPEII. FEATURES TYPICAL OF ROMAN GARDENS
INCLUDE THE PERGOLAS AND THE LATTICE-WORK USED TO DIVIDE
INDIVIDUAL GARDENS.

GERTRUDE JEKYLL (1843-1932)

Born in Victorian England, Gertrude Jekyll grew up in a cultured middle-class home and, for her generation, received a superior education with a very gifted governess who taught her botany and painting. With considerable artistic talent she went at the age of 17 to Kensington School of Art. In her early twenties she travelled to France, Italy and Greece, and by the time the family was settled in a newly built home in Surrey she had a considerable reputation as an artist and craftswoman, and her wide circle of friends included John Ruskin and Edward Burne Jones.

In 1891 her sight began to deteriorate, and she could no longer paint or do the embroidery for which she was famous. Her great consolation was her gardening.

It was at this time that she met the young architect Edwin Lutyens. She was 50, he was 22. It was the beginning of an artistic partnership. Lutyens designed her new house at Munstead on land where Gertrude had already established a garden. She had already published two books on gardening and contributed regularly to gardening periodicals.

Influenced by Monet, she could be described as an Impressionist gardener. English gardeners at this time were still influenced by the French formal garden, but she was a flower gardener with the artists' love of colour guiding the gardener's skill. It was at this time too that William Robinson, author of 'The English Flower Garden', and friend of Gertrude Jekyll, introduced the herbaceous border.

She designed garden tools which were made up by the local blacksmith. For the rest of her life she collaborated with Lutyens, designed gardens for his houses – 'a Lutyens house with a Jekyll garden'.

One of her most general ideas about the use of colour is that flowers which bloom at the same time should be arranged where possible close to each other. It is better, she thought, to have a clump of colour at one time of the year and then a space of green to follow than to have bits of colour dotted about so that there is always something in flower in a particular bed or border of the garden.

I went to Lordship's when I was fourteen and stayed for fourteen years. There were seven gardeners and goodness knows how many servants in the house. It was a frightening experience for a boy. Lord and Ladyship were very, very Victorian and very domineering. It was 'swing your arms' every time they saw us. Ladyship would appear suddenly from nowhere when one of us boys were walking off to fetch something. 'Swing your arms!' she would shout. We wore green baize aprons and collars and ties, no matter how hot it was, and whatever we had to do had to be done on the dot. Nobody was allowed to smoke. A gardener was immediately sacked if he was caught smoking, no matter how long he had worked there.

We must never be seen from the house; it was forbidden. And if people were sitting on the terrace or on the lawn, and you had a great barrow-load of weeds, you might have to push it as much as a mile to keep out of view. If you were seen you were always told about it and warned, and as you walked away Ladyship would call after you, 'Swing your arms!'. It was terrible. You felt like somebody with a disease.

The boy under-gardeners had to help arrange the flowers in the house. These were done every day. We had to creep in early in the morning before breakfast and replace great banks of flowers in the main rooms. Lordship and Ladyship must never hear or see you doing it; fresh flowers had to just be there, that was all there was to it. There was never a dead flower. It was as if flowers, for them, lived for ever. It was part of the magic in their lives. But the arrangements were how they wanted them and if one of the gardeners had used his imagination, Ladyship noticed at once and soon put a stop to it! The guests always complimented her on the flowers and she always accepted the praise as though she had grown, picked and arranged them herself. It was logical because servants were just part of the machinery of the big house and people don't thank machines, they just keep them trim and working. Or that's how I look at it.

As the years went by, we young men found ourselves being able to talk to Lordship and Ladyship. 'Never speak to them — not one word and no matter how urgent — until they speak to you,' the head-gardener told me on my first day. Ladyship drove about the grounds in a motor-chair and would have run us over rather than have to say, 'get out the way'. We must never look at her and

NUTHILL HOUSE AND GARDEN 1853 COMBINES THREE STYLES —
VICTORIAN, GARDENESQUE AND LANDSCAPE DESIGN.

she never looked at us. It was the same in the house. If a maid was in a passage and Lordship or Ladyship happened to come along, she would have to face the wall and stand perfectly still until they had passed. I wouldn't think that they felt anything about their servants. We were just there because we were necessary, like water from the tap. We had to listen for voices. If we heard them in a certain walk, we had to make a detour, if not it was, 'But why weren't you listening?' and 'Be alert, boy!' and, when you had been dismissed, 'Swing your arms!' The garden was huge. The pleasure grounds alone, and not including the park, covered seven acres. The kind of gardening we did there is not seen nowadays. It was a perfect art. Topiary, there was a lot of that. It was a very responsible job.

You had only to make one bad clip and a pheasant became a duck. The gardeners usually made up these creatures themselves. We were tempted to cut out something terrible sometimes, so that it grew and grew . . . but of course we never did. Even when we went on to mechanical hedge-trimmers we still kept on topiary. There was a great pride in it, and in hedge-cutting of every sort. It was the hedge which set the garden off and all the big houses competed with each other. Fences were marvellous things, too; there were more than two miles of them round Lordship's and not a pale which wasn't exact. The hedges had tops like billiard-tables. It was get down and have a look, and stand back and have a look. No hedge was left until it was marvellous. There were so many things which really had no need to be done but which we did out of a kind of obstinate pleasure. The asparagus beds in winter were an example. We'd spend hours getting the sides of the clamps absolutely flat and absolutely at a 45° angle, although an ordinary heap of earth would have done just as well.

None of the village people was allowed into the garden. Definitely not. Trades-people came to their door and never saw the main gardens. Work in front of the house had to be done secretly. About seven in the morning we would tiptoe about the terrace, sweeping the leaves, tying things up, never making a sound, so that nobody in the bedrooms could hear the work being done. This is what luxury means — perfect consideration. We gave, they took. It was the complete arrangement. This is luxury.

Of course, they spent a terrific amount of money on the house and garden. It was the machinery they had to have in order to live. So they kept it going, as you

FOUR GARDENS OF FORMAL BEDS ENCLOSED BY THICK HEDGES, THESE
ARE SURROUNDED BY A WOODEN FENCE AND, SURROUNDING THE
WHOLE ARE ELABORATE ARBORS OR GALLERIES.

might say. A bad servant was just a bad part and was exchanged for a good part as soon as possible. I thought of this when I was doing my National Service as a fitter in the R.A.C. It made sense. Yet I got so that I didn't know quite what to think about it all. It was obviously wrong, yet because Lordship and Ladyship were old and had never known any other kind of life, I suppose I felt sorry for them. I always had to give more than was necessary. I couldn't resist it. It was exciting somehow. But when I got home I would be angry with myself. The butler would sometimes come to the pub and imitate them. Laugh — you should have heard us! But I would feel strange inside, pitying and hating at the same time. His favourite joke was:

Ladyship: 'Shall we ask the So-and-Sos to luncheon, Bertie?'
Silence, then, 'Can they play bridge? Will they like my garden?'
Ladyship: 'No, I don't think so.'
Lordship: 'Then don't have'em.'

Lordship was a friend of King George V. He was a terribly nice man — a real gentleman. A lot of royalty came down from time to time and Lordship and Ladyship were sometimes at Sandringham. The Queen (Queen Elizabeth the Queen Mother) came. She treated us very well and loved the garden. She would tell us boys what they ate for luncheon and then we'd all laugh. The Princess Royal was just the same — easy. But Members of Parliament always imitated Lordship and Ladyship and treated us like fittings. I was amazed by the Royalty. I imagined a bigger kind of Ladyship, but definitely not.

It was strange coming back to the big house after the R.A.C. I was married now and we had an estate cottage without inside water, a bath or electricity, although it was very pretty and we were very happy. At first, that is. Until Ladyship said that my wife must work in the big house. My wife didn't understand what it would mean. She came from Ilford and had never seen anything like it. She got worried and then she got migraine. The doctor told her that she must leave her work at the big house because it was making her anxious and ill. I told Ladyship, who said, 'But she must come.' I told her what the doctor had said but she just drove to the cottage and told my wife, 'You must come back to the kitchen — do you understand? You must.' So that is why we went away. I felt sorry for my wife and for Ladyship; they had no way of knowing each other.

A GARDEN SCENE BY THOMAS ROBINS THE ELDER C.1750,
SHOWING SCYTHING, ROLLING AND RAKING TO KEEP THE LAWN IN
TRIM.

*The big house helped me in my life and changed me. Being in private service has
educated me. I can talk to anybody. There is one thing about Suffolk and that is
that they find talk terribly difficult. I don't. I have learned to talk. But working
for Lordship made me a foreigner in the village. Those who remain with their
own calibre in the village stay in the village family. I belonged to the big-house
family and it was hard to leave. I saw the last of the big house while it was self-
supporting. Everything, milk, cream, butter, game, fish, flowers, chicory, endive,
melons, they were all there behind the hedges. Whatever Lordship and Ladyship
wished for, they asked for, and it was brought.*

RONALD BLYTHE'S PORTRAIT OF A SUFFOLK VILLAGE FROM AKENFIELD — 1967.
THIS MAN (CHRISTOPHER FALCONER) WAS 39 AT THE TIME OF THIS RECORD.

IN THE GARDEN

DESIGN FOR A MAZE FROM 'THE PROFITABLE ART OF GARDENING' 1568.

— MAZES, KNOTS AND WALKS —

A particularly delightful feature of earlier gardens, the maze, has all but disappeared, and it is said that there are fewer than a dozen in existence. The most familiar is the yew-hedge maze. They were fashionable in Tudor times, and it is possible that the 'boxwood hedge' in 'Twelfth Night', where Malvolio found Maria's letter, might have been the garden maze. Many people are familiar with the maze at Hampton Court, created in the time of Queen Anne; there is one in the private garden of Hatfield House, another at Chatsworth. It is doubtful if any of these are as they were originally created, while the Chatsworth maze is a new one, planted comparatively recently. The explanation for their decline is simple; they needed to be trimmed expertly by hand, a seemingly never-ending task, and without unlimited labour their maintenance became an expensive burden. Some of the mazes were intricate, and anyone unable to find his way out would solve the problem by breaking through the hedge. The unfortunate gardener would then have to repair the maze by planting fresh shrubs. One can understand why the owners rarely allow members of the public to explore the maze.

Another kind of maze, the turf maze, is of ancient origin. These are not found in gardens but as part of the play area of the village green. They are usually circular, and made by raised turf forming an intricate path which stands above the gravel. Titania, in 'A Midsummer Night's Dream', speaks of their neglect:

> 'The quaint mazes in the wanton green
> For lack of tread are indistinguishable'.

It is thought that these turf-mazes have their origin in a similar circular pattern found in the tiles of a monastery floor, where they became 'prayer-walks' for monks telling their beads.

There is a well-maintained turf-maze by the roadside at the village of Wing in Rutland. A resident explained that in his childhood he was sent to walk the maze as a punishment for being naughty.

17TH CENTURY MOUNTS
IN THE GROUNDS OF NEW COLLEGE, OXFORD.

◇

Here by the waye (gentle Reader) I doe place two proper Mazes . . . as proper adournements upon pleasure to a Garden, that who that listeth (havinge such rowme in their Garden) may place the one of them (which liketh them beste) in that voyde place of The Garden, that may best be spared (for the onely purpose) to sporte them in at times, which mazis being workmanly handled by the Gardiner, he shall beutyfye them much, in divising foure sundry fruites to be placed in eche of the corners of the maze, and in the middle of it maye be a proper herber decked with roses to be set or els a faire tree of Rosemary, or other fruyt, at the discretion of the Gardiner'.

FROM THE PROFITABLE ART OF GARDENING (1568)

◇

Hyll gives two designs for mazes. To modern ears the word maze generally suggests a hedge-maze, but with few exceptions the mazes described by writers in Elizabethan and Stuart days were the low-growing shrub mazes; made, as Hyll suggests, of hyssop, lavender cotton, wintry savory or thyme, and in the small garden which Hyll describes such a maze would have been both delightful and in keeping with it surroundings. One cannot help wondering where Hyll obtained these two designs, for curiously enough, exactly the same mazes are depicted in Du Cerceau's plan for the great parterre at the Chateau de Gaillon, the most magnificent Country residence in France in the early sixteenth century.

FROM ELEANOUR SINCLAIR ROHDE — THE OLD ENGLISH GARDENING BOOKS.

◇

Mounts

Miles Hadfield, in his 'History of British Gardening' gives a remarkable description of the mount which was built for Henry VIII in 1533:

'Upon a foundation of over a quarter million bricks soil was piled, and planted with hawthorns. On the summit stood a many-windowed three-storeyed building, roofed with a lead cupola surmounted by a vane in the form of a heraldic lion. This 'lantern arbour' was reached by a pathway spiralling up like the turnings of cockle-shells, bordered by heraldic beasts carved in stone.

The mount was to be a feature of large gardens until late in the following century. It took various forms, but in principle seems always to have consisted of some kind of arbour raised on a pile of earth above the general level of the garden to 'a pretty height', so that, having spiralled up, one might look abroad into the fields and over one's domain. The mount was planted with clipped shrubs, or perhaps low box hedges, which bordered the ascending path'.

As for the making of knots or figures, with divers coloured earths that they may lie under the windows of the house on that side which the garden stands, They be but toys; you may see as good sights many times in tarts.

FRANCIS BACON — 'OF GARDENS' 1625

By the entrance I noticed numerous patches where square cavities had been scooped out as for paving stones; some of these were filled with red brick-dust, some with white sand, and some with green lawn, very much resembling a chessboard.

THOMAS PLATT, A GERMAN, DESCRIBING THE KNOT GARDEN AT HAMPTON COURT 1599

THE FAMOUS STONE GARDEN AT RYOAN-JI,
KYOTO

In The Garden

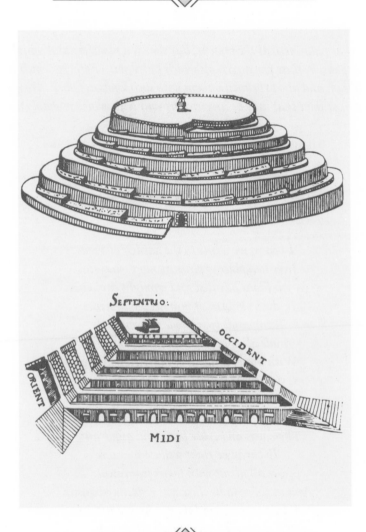

FRENCH DESIGNS FOR MOUNTS 1603.
TOP: A SIX-STAGE SPIRAL, AND BELOW, A SQUARE DESIGN IN WHICH THE
TERRACES WERE USED TO GROW HERBS.

45

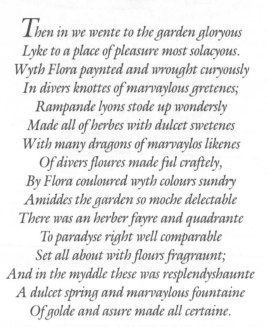

But what remaineth at the present, but that you modelize and contrive your Garden plots, by these few directions which I give you, or others, which you may better like of; and also to beautifie them with such knots as follow hereafter of my invention, or those that may be invented by your selfe, which probably may please your fancy better than mine.

STEPHEN BLAKE — *THE COMPLEAT GARDENER'S PRACTICE. 1664*

Then in we wente to the garden gloryous
Lyke to a place of pleasure most solacyous.
Wyth Flora paynted and wrought curyously
In divers knottes of marvaylous gretenes;
Rampande lyons stode up wondersly
Made all of herbes with dulcet swetenes
With many dragons of marvaylos likenes
Of divers floures made ful craftely,
By Flora couloured wyth colours sundry
Amiddes the garden so moche delectable
There was an herber fayre and quadrante
To paradyse right well comparable
Set all about with flours fragraunt;
And in the myddle these was resplendyshaunte
A dulcet spring and marvaylous fountaine
Of golde and asure made all certaine.

STEPHEN HAWES — *THE HISTORY OF GRAND AMOUR AND BELL PUCELLE 1509*
(CONSIDERED TO BE A DESCRIPTION OF HENRY VII'S GARDEN AT RICHMOND)

———◇———

My gardens sweet, enclosed with walles strong
Enbanked with benches to sytt and take my rest
The Knotts so enknotted, it cannot be exprest
With arbors and alys so plesaunt and so dulce,
The pestylent ayers with flavors to repulse.

THOMAS (OR GEORGE) CAVENDISH — *MEMOIRS OF CARDINAL WOLSEY* — (c1532)

———◇———

———◇———

DESIGN FOR A MAZE FROM 'THE PROFITABLE ART OF GARDENING' 1568.

———◇———

---

*A*mong other things discussed of the present fashion of gardens to make them plain that we have the best walks of gravel in the world. France having none, nor Italy; and the green of our bowling-alleys is better than any they have. So our business here being air, this is the best way, only with a little mixture of statues, or pots, which may be handsome, and so filled with another pot of such and such a flower or green, as the season of the year will bear. And then for flowers, they are best seen in a little plot by themselves: besides, their borders spoil the walks of another garden; and then for fruit, the best way is to have walls built circularly one within another, to the south, on purpose for fruit, and leave the walking garden only for that use.

SAMUEL PEPYS — IN CONVERSATION WITH HUGH MAY, COMPTROLLER OF THE WORKS, 1666. (MAY HAD CONSIDERABLE INFLUENCE ON THE ARCHITECTURE OF THE DAY.)

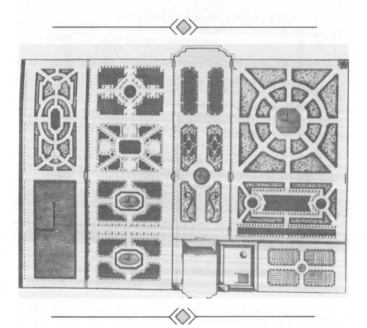

THIS PLAN OF A 20-ACRE GARDEN INCLUDES THE FIRST KNOWN ENGLISH

REPRESENTATION OF A HA-HA (TOP CENTRE).

THE SCENTED GARDEN

Yet the rose has one powerful virtue to boast,
Above all the flowers of the field
When its leaves are all dead and fine colours are lost,
Still how sweet a perfume it will yield.

ISAAC WATTS 1674-1748

The 'Precious Ointment' of the scriptures was a compound of olive oil, myrrh,
cassia, cinnamon and sweet calamus. It was a sacred production, and could not
be used for secular purposes. A precious ointment is still used for the Pope's
Golden Rose. In the early Christian Church not only incense but the oil of the
lamps, and even the wax of the tapers were perfumed.
In 370BC Theophrastus wrote a work on fragrant plants in which he says
'Perfumes are made from Roses, White Lilies and Violets, some from stalks and
some from roots.
Horace was very fond of flowers and perfumes. In his ode celebrating the return
of Augustus from Spain he bids the slaves get rarest perfumes, and especially
desires the tuneful Neaera to make haste and knot up her scented hair.
In the thirteenth century the Doge of Venice might receive no presents of gifts
from anyone, except offerings of rosewater, leaves, flowers and sweet herbs.
Gervase Markham in 1647 published his 'The English Housewife' which treats
specially with 'Conceited Secrets, distillations and perfumes'. It contains recipes
for perfuming gloves and jerkins and for the making of perfumes to burn, for
pomanders and for sweets bagges, and Damask water.

F W BURBIDGE — THE BOOK OF THE SCENTED GARDEN

Perfume starts in the green parts of the plant, and its ingredients are light from the sun, carbon dioxide from the air, and the plant's own water . . .

The workings of the plant's perfumery in making sufficient raw materials in its green parts, conveying them to the petals on schedule, and conducting an intricate laboratory process within a swiftly growing and fragile material are marvellous indeed. The perfumery is only one industry within the green skin of a plant, for also in the making are colours and pollen and ovules, to name but a few, all to be initiated and placed in working order at precise times and places. . .

Efforts have been made to analyse rose perfumes, which is an interesting study with some long words in it. But when we come down to it, all that matters to us right now is to know which are the most fragrant roses for our enjoyment . . . I will give you mine by sweetness more than by strength.

JACK HARKNESS — ROSES.

THE MOSS ROSE,
A FLOWER POPULAR IN THE LATE 18TH CENTURY.

The most fragrant twenty roses
chosen by Jack Harkness

Lady Penzance	Eglanteria Hybrid
Alec's Red	Hybrid Tea
Fragrant Cloud	Hybrid Tea
Margaret Merril	Floribunda
Polly	Hybrid Tea
Boule de Neige	Bourbon
Crimson Glory	Climbing Hybrid Tea
Konigin von Danemark	Alba
Ophelia	Hybrid Tea
Scabrosa	Rugosa Hybrid
Belle de Crecy	Gallica
Blue Moon	Hybrid Tea
Compassion	Climbing Hybrid Tea
Etoile de Holland	Climbing Hybrid Tea
Mme Gregoire Staechelin	Climbing Hybrid Tea
Mme Pierre Oger	Bourbon
Mrs John Laing	Hybrid Perpetual
President Herbert Hoover	Hybrid Tea
Sutter's Gold	Hybrid Tea
Whiskey Mac	Hybrid Tea

Soon will the high Midsummer pomps come on,
Soon will the musk carnations break and swell,
Soon shall we have gold-dusted snap dragon,
Sweet William with his homely cottage smell,
And stock in fragrant blow.

MATTHEW ARNOLD — THYRSIS

Pot-pourri

The making of Pot-pourri by Gertrude Jekyll's method requires a large floor-space, a team of helpers to be rewarded afterwards with tea, and bushels of flowers. She had a specially made cask, which would hold fifteen gallons of the finished (wet) pot-pourri. When finished, the cask weighed nearly two hundredweights. She had two recipes, one for dry pot-pourri, the other for the moist, which she preferred. There are simpler recipes:

An Essex recipe

Making pot-pourri is a pleasant, relaxing pursuit with an end product that can be used for many years. It will scent rooms, keep luggage and vehicles country fresh, banish dog and cat smells, help to bring gentle sleep and even discourage tiresome insects.

Rose petals are the favourite ingredient, and the most fragrant should be chosen, together with sweet geranium leaves, lavender, sweet verbena, camomile flowers, lemon verbena and marigolds. Smaller quantities of thyme, rosemary, bay, sweet basil and mint may be included. Petals of sweet peas and delphiniums are included to add colour to the mixture.

Pinks and carnations are sweetly scented but the petals are too small to be effective.

Gather plant material on a morning when there is no moisture in the air. Pull the petals and the leaves apart and spread them loosely on paper in a warm airy place. A spare bedroom floor with the window slightly open is a good drying place. This will take between three to seven days. Afterwards store the dried material in an airtight tin in a dry cupboard until you have time to use it. When you are ready, add a few drops of an essential oil (roses of Florence is good) and about a teaspoon of orris-root powder as a fixative to every five handfuls of dried petals and leaves. Spices, though not essential, give a special 'tang' if you add about a teaspoon of crushed cinnamon, grated nutmeg, or dried cloves.

Mix thoroughly and store in jars with tight fitting lids. The jars should be nearly full, but allow a small space so that the mixture can be given a good shake every day for several weeks. The finished pot-pourri will last for years.

TITLE PAGE OF 'THE SECOND PART OF THE GARDENERS LABYRINTH'.

A simple recipe from Australia

Rose petals (gathered when the flowers are in full bloom but not falling) lemon verbena, lavender, scented thyme and any other fragrant flowers, — honeysuckle, frangipani, carnation, gardenia etc.

Dry indoors on a sunny window sill where the air can play on them. Stir frequently. When they are completey dry, add spices in the following proportions:

1 oz bay salt

½ oz cloves

½ oz cinnamon

½ oz allspice

1 oz orris root, powdered

a grain or two of musk

Stir well and place in a jar with a lid.

And because the breath of flowers is far sweeter in the air (where it comes and goes, like the warbling of music) than in the hand, therefore nothing is more fit for that delight, than to know what be the flowers and plants that do best perfume the air. Roses, damask and red, are fast flowers of their smells; so that you may walk by a whole row of them, and find nothing of their sweetness; yea, though it be in a morning's dew. Bays likewise yield no smell as they grow. Rosemary little; nor sweet marjoram. That which above all others yields the sweetest smell in the air, is the violet; specially the white double violet, which comes twice a year; about the middle of April, and about Bartholomewtide. Next to that is the musk-rose. Then the strawberry-leaves dying, which [yield] a most excellent cordial smell. Then the flower of the vines; it is a little dust, like the dust of a bent [grass], which grows upon the cluster in the first coming forth. Then sweet briar. Then wallflowers, which are very delightful to be set under a parlour or lower chamber window. Then pinks and gilly flowers, specially the matted pink and clove gillyflower. Then the flowers of the lime tree. Then the honeysuckles, so they be somewhat afar off. Of bean flowers I speak not, because they are field flowers. But those which perfume the air most delightfully, not passed by as the rest, but being trodden upon and crushed, are three: that is, burnet, wild thyme, and water mints. Therefore you are to set whole alleys of them, to have the pleasure when you walk or tread.

FRANCIS BACON — OF GARDENS.

A VASE AND ARCH TERMINATING A VISTA THROUGH TO THE PADDOCK
AT DRAYTON GREEN.

An Alphabet of scented flowers and leaves

Acacia farnesiana	*Lilac*
The Australian mimosa	*Lilium candidum*
Ageratum	*Lily of the Valley*
Basil	*Mignonette*
Bergamot	*Mint*
Begonia	*Myrtle*
Carnation	*Narcissus*
Camomile	*Nicotiana*
Citrus aurantium	*Night Scented Stock*
Daphne	*Oenothera (Evening Primrose)*
Dianthus	*Origanum (Marjoram)*
Eucalyptus	*Petunia*
Frangipani	*Philadelphus*
Freesia	*Rosemary*
Gardenia	*Rose*
Geranium	*Rocket (Sweet Rocket — Hesperis matronalis)*
Hawthorne	*Scabious*
Heliotrope	*Sweet Pea*
Honeysuckle	*Tansy*
Hyacinth	*Thyme*
Iberis oderatoa	*Vibernum*
Jasmine	*Violet*
Jonquil	*Wallflower*
Laurus nobilis (Sweet Bay)	*Wintersweet*
Lavender	*Wisteria*
	Yarrow

THIS 15TH CENTURY GARDENER IS WORKING WITH A LONG-HANDLED,
SLIGHTLY SCOOPED WOODEN SPADE. THE PLOT IS ENCLOSED BY A
STRONG WOODEN FENCE. THE DEEP RAISED BEDS INCLUDE TWO
STANDARD ROSES WITH HORIZONTAL "WHEEL" SUPPORTS.

Through the open windows also, at almost anytime of the year, pours the delicious scent of leaf and flower — of Winter Sweet, Violets or Sweet Peas; of Stocks or Mignonette; of Wallflowers, or Roses. Just to name a few of the plants whose scent fills the rooms, what glories are thereby called up — Honeysuckle and Jasmine, Lily of the Valley, Lilac and Narcissus, Carnation, Syringa and Heliotrope, Thyme, Bergamot and Aloysia!

These and a hundred other fragrances mingled together in infinitely varying combinations, give sensuous joys which even the most jaded can but appreciate. For there is probably no pleasure so democratic as that which is yielded by the fragrance of flowers and leaves. The colour and form of plants require a little attention for their appreciation, but their odour overwhelms our senses whether we attend or no. The variety of perfumes yielded by plants is almost as great as their forms, for blossom of Apple and of Jonquil, leaf of Strawberry, Currant and Sweet Gale gives each an aesthetic pleasure peculiar to itself

HARRY ROBERTS — THE BOOK OF OLD FASHIONED FLOWERS (1901).

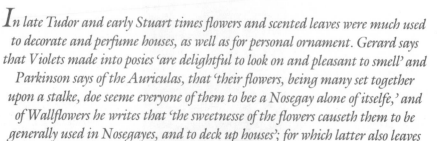

In late Tudor and early Stuart times flowers and scented leaves were much used to decorate and perfume houses, as well as for personal ornament. Gerard says that Violets made into posies 'are delightful to look on and pleasant to smell' and Parkinson says of the Auriculas, that 'their flowers, being many set together upon a stalke, doe seeme everyone of them to bee a Nosegay alone of itselfe,' and of Wallflowers he writes that 'the sweetnesse of the flowers causeth them to be generally used in Nosegayes, and to deck up houses'; for which latter also leaves and branches of box 'serve both summer and winter'. Scented flowers and herbs were also extensively used, together with coarser herbage, for the strawing and strewing of floors; and Parkinson mentions germander as being 'much used as a strawing herbe for houses, being pretty and sweete.'

HARRY ROBERTS — ENGLISH GARDENS.

To distil rose water: Gather your red roses when they are dry and full blown, pick off the leaves, and to every peck put one quart of water, then put them into a cold still, and make a slow fire under it, the slower you distil it the better it is, then bottle it, and cork it in two or three day's time, (and) keep it for use.

NB. You may distil bean flowers the same way.

If your still be a limbeck, when you set it on fill the top with cold water, and make a little paste of flour and water and close the bottom of your still well with it, and take great care that your fire is not too hot to make it boil over, for that will weaken the strength of your water; you must change the water on the top of your still often, and never let it be scalding hot, and your still will drop gradually off; if you use a hot still, when you put on the top, dip a cloth in white lead and oil, and lay it well over the edges of your still, and a coarse wet cloth over the top; it requires a little fire under it, but you must take care that you keep it very clear; when your cloth is dry, dip it in cold water and lay it on again, and if your still be hot, wet another cloth, and lay it round the top, and keep it of a moderate heat so that your water is cold when it comes off the still.

FROM *THE EXPERIENCED HOUSEKEEPER*, BY ELIZABETH RAFFOLD — 1787
(HOUSEKEEPER TO THE HON LADY ELIZABETH WARBURTON).

INTERIOR OF A STILL ROOM FROM 'THE FRENCH GARDINER' (1691).

FLOWERS
AND
PLANTS

Here's flowers for you:
Hot lavender, mints, savory, marjoram,
The marigold that goes to bed with the sun
And with him rises weeping . . . daffodils
That come before the swallow dares, and take
The winds of March with beauty; violets dim
But sweeter than the lids of Juno's eyes
Or Cytherea's breath; pale primroses
That die unmarried, ere they can behold
Bright Phoebus in his strength
bold oxlips and
The crown imperial; lilies of all kinds,
The flower de luce being one.

SHAKESPEARE — WINTER'S TALE

'At the first planting of the Royal garden in St James Park, a great number of
acacias were planted in the walks that M Mollet (one of the king's French
gardeners) then made; but in a few years they were all cut down, by reason of the
least gust of wind broke some of their branches.'

SAMUEL PEPYS — DIARY. COMMENTS ON CHARLES II'S
PLANS TO REDESIGN ST JAMES'S PARK.

Plants to be found in an Elizabethan garden:

Roses, snapdragons, sweet williams, honeysuckle, carnations, pinks, pansies, wallflowers, hollyhocks, columbines, cowslips, lilies, lilies of the valley, crown imperial, daffodils, lavender, peonies, poppies, marigolds, primroses, violets, valerian.

◇

Flowers worthy of paradise . . .
Flowers of all hue, and without thorn the rose.

MILTON — PARADISE LOST

◇

The English Flower garden may afford far greater pleasure than it does at present. We must learn to look on plants not as mere points of colour, but as old friends on whose coming we can rely, and who, returning with the recurring seasons, bring back with them pleasant memories of past years.'

HENRY BRIGHT — ENGLISH FLOWER GARDEN 1881

◇

And 'tis my faith that every flower
Enjoys the air it breathes

WORDSWORTH — LINES WRITTEN IN EARLY SPRING

◇

No garden without its weeds.

◇

Flowers have an expression of countenance as much as men or animals. Some seem to smile; some have a sad expression; some are pensive and diffident; others again are plain, honest and upright, like the broad faced sunflower and the hollyhock.

HENRY WARD BEECHER

Shed no tear! O shed no tear!
The flowers will bloom another year.
Weep no more! O weep no more!
Young buds sleep in the root's white core.

KEATS — FAERY SONG

THE PREPARATION AND DISTILLING OF HERBS IN A PHYSIC GARDEN 1531.

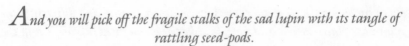

And you will pick off the fragile stalks of the sad lupin with its tangle of rattling seed-pods.

VIRGIL — GEORGICS I 75

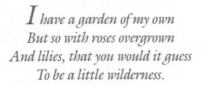

I have a garden of my own
But so with roses overgrown
And lilies, that you would it guess
To be a little wilderness.

ANDREW MARVELL

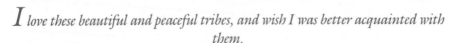

I love these beautiful and peaceful tribes, and wish I was better acquainted with them.

W S LANDER — IN A LETTER, REFERRING TO FLOWERS

As for marigolds, poppies, hollyhocks, and valorous sunflowers, we shall never have a garden without them, both for their own sake, and for the sake of old fashioned folks, who used to love them.

HENRY WARD BEECHER — A DISCOURSE OF FLOWERS

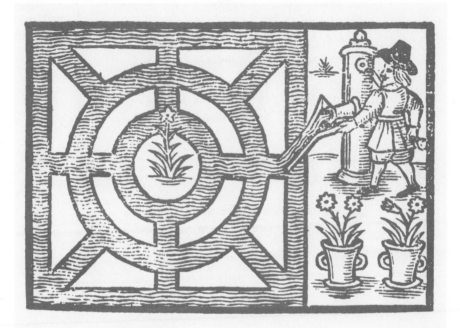

'A GARDENERS LABYRINTH'

The fairest flowers soonest fade.
PROVERB

To create a little flower is the labour of ages.
WILLIAM BLAKE

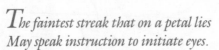

See how the flowers, as at parade,
Under their colours stand displayed:
Each regiment in order grows,
That of the tulip, pink and rose.

ANDREW MARVELL

The faintest streak that on a petal lies
May speak instruction to initiate eyes.

BRYANT — THE MYSTERY OF FLOWERS

Here in this sequestered close
Bloom the hyacinth and rose;
Here beside the modest stock
Flaunts the flaming holly hock;
Here, without a pang, one sees
Ranks, conditions, and degrees.

AUSTIN DOBSON — A GARDEN SONG

Full many a flower is born to blush unseen
And waste its sweetness on the desert air.

GRAY — ELEGY IN A COUNTRY CHURCHYARD

Flowers that their gay wardrobe wear.

MILTON — *LYCIDAS*

*Mary, Mary, quite contrary
How does your garden grow?
With silver bells, and cockle shells,
And pretty maids all in a row.*

NURSERY RHYME

Earth laughs in flowers.

EMERSON

TITLE PAGE OF 'A NEW ORCHARD AND GARDEN'.

Speak not – whisper not:
Here groweth thyme and bergamot; . . .
Dark-spiked rosemary and myrrh
Lean stalked, purple lavender.

WALTER DE LA MARE — THE SUNKEN GARDEN

The tufted basil, pun-provoking thyme,
Fresh balm, and marigold of cheerful hue.

WILLIAM SHENSTONE

There's rosemary, that's for remembrance; pray, love, remember: and there is
pansies, that's for thoughts . . . There's fennel for you, and columbines; there's
rue for you; and here's some for me . . . There's a daisy: I would give you some
violets, but they withered all when my father died.

SHAKESPEARE — HAMLET (OPHELIA)

Culpepper, the man that first ranged the woods and climbed the mountains in
search of medicinal and salutary herbs, has undoubtedly merited the gratitude
of posterity.

DR JOHNSON

PICTORIAL PLAN OF A GARDEN FROM 'A NEW ORCHARD AND GARDEN'.

Beware the Artichoke

Known in the seventeenth century as Canadian potatoes – 'Put into seething water they are soon boiled tender which after they bee peeled, sliced and stewed in butter and a little wine was a dish for a Queene' But 'which way soever they be drest and eaten, they stirre up and cause a filthie loathesome stinking winde within the bodie thereby causing the belly to be pained and tormented'.

The globe artichoke was a popular delicacy in the seventeenth century, and those grown in England were considered superior to those grown in Europe.

Sunflowers were used in a similar way, the immature flower buds were cooked and eaten with butter, vinegar and pepper, and one writer noted that they were 'exceedingly pleasant meate surpassing the artichoke far in procuring bodily lust'.

―――――◇―――――

Artochoke reformeth the savour of the mouth
Artochoke causeth urine and the veneriall act
Artochoke amendeth the hardness of making water and the rank savour
of the armpits
Artochoke strengtheneth the stomacke, and helpeth the privie places that men
children may be conceived.

THOMAS HYLL — THE GARDENER'S LABYRINTH

―――――◇―――――

The Vine

In the Middle Ages vineyards had been associated with the monasteries, and those at Ely had attained fame. Plat (1594) charges the disappearance of vineyards to ignorance. Parkinson explained, however, that 'the wine of late made hath been but small and not durable like that which cometh from beyond the sea, whether our unkindly years or the want of skill or a convenient place for a vineyard be the cause I cannot well tell you'.

VINE HERBER FROM 'THE GARDENERS LABYRINTH'.

A SOURCE OF INFINITE PLEASURE

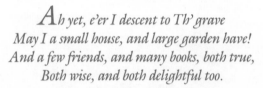

Ah yet, e'er I descent to Th' grave
May I a small house, and large garden have!
And a few friends, and many books, both true,
Both wise, and both delightful too.

ABRAHAM COWLEY

To own a bit of ground, to scratch it with a hoe, to plant seeds and watch the
renewal of life – this is the commonest delight of the race, the most satisfactory
thing a man can do.

CHARLES DUDLEY WARNER (1829-1900) — MY SUMMER IN A GARDEN

No man but feels more of a man in the world if he have but a bit of ground
that he can call his own. However small it is on the surface, it is four thousand
miles deep; and that is a very handsome property.

CHARLES DUDLEY WARNER (1829-1900)

Freshly turved
And shapen was this herber, roof and all.
As is a pretty parlour; and also
The hegge as thick as is a castle wall,
So that who list without to stand or go,
Though he would all day prien to and fro,
He shoulde not see if there were any wighte
Within or no; but one within well mighte
Perceive alle that yeden there withoute.

CHAUCER — THE FLOWER & THE LEAF

A MEDIEVAL GARDENER.

The Hanging Gardens of Babylon

About the 5th century BC the Babylonian king Nebuchadnezzar married the Median Princess Amytis. She was soon homesick for the green hills and trees of her native land. To gratify her, the king built a huge structure 400ft square on the west bank of the River Euphrates. In the crowded city of Babylon it rose as a pyramid to the height of 100ft and was one of the seven wonders of the world.

The various terraces were made of cement and great sheets of lead to protect the walls of the building from the moisture that seeped from above.

'On this was spread deep rich loam, and therein were planted . . . rare flowers and shrubs that delighted with colour and perfume . . . and the broadleaf trees grew into stately dimensons and clung to the breast of the nurse as trustfully as if it had been Mother Earth herself.'

―◇―

Be still. The Hanging Gardens were a dream.
TRUMBULL STICKNEY 1905

―◇―

A garden is like those pernicious machineries which catch a man's coat-skirt or his hand, and draw in his arm, his leg, and his whole body to irresistible destruction.
EMERSON — CONDUCT OF LIFE

―◇―

Who loves a garden still his Eden keeps,
Perennial pleasures plants, and wholesome harvests reaps.

A B ALCOTT

Gardens were before gardeners, and but some hours after the earth.

SIR THOMAS BROWNE 1658

Show me your garden and I shall tell you what you are.

ALFRED AUSTIN 1905

THESE 17TH CENTURY PROPAGATORS ARE CLEFT-GRAFTING. THE
INCISION IS MADE WITH A THICK KNIFE AND A MALLET.

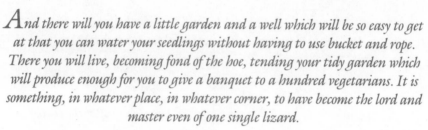

And there will you have a little garden and a well which will be so easy to get at that you can water your seedlings without having to use bucket and rope. There you will live, becoming fond of the hoe, tending your tidy garden which will produce enough for you to give a banquet to a hundred vegetarians. It is something, in whatever place, in whatever corner, to have become the lord and master even of one single lizard.

JUVENAL (60-140 AD) — SATIRE III

All that in this delightful garden grows
Should happy be, and have immortal bliss.

SPENSER

. . . My craving for rest is such that twenty years would hardly serve to satisfy me, and that is ten more than I am likely to live — a soldier nowadays is old at forty. . . . why, gardening has become so interesting to me here, as to force me to give it up, lest neglect of business should follow: it is a kind of madness with me. Gardening from morning to night should be my occupation if there was anyone to command the regiment, it won't let me think of anything else. So hang the garden, and the sweet red and blue birds that swarm around: and hang Dame Nature for making me love such things, and women's company, more than the sublime pleasure of cutting people's throats, and teaching young men to do so.

CHARLES NAPIER — IN A LETTER TO HIS MOTHER 1813

Man was lost and saved in a garden.
PASCAL — PENSÉES

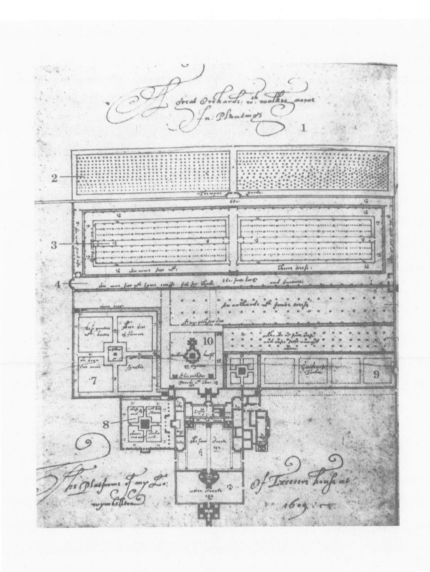

JOHN SMYTHSON'S PLAN OF WIMBLEDON GARDENS 1609.

A Royal Welcome

When Queen Elizabeth visited the Earl of Hertford in September 1591 she was met by six garlanded girls and led to a miniature crescent-shaped lake, scooped out in honour of Her Majesty's arrival; but en route the royal carriage was stopped by country people who showered their sovereign with flowers and gave her nosegays picked from their own yards.

My master hath a garden, full filled with divers flowers,
Where Thou mayst gather posies gay, all times and hours,
Here naught is heard
But paradise-bird
Harp dulcimer and lute
With cymbal,
And timbrel,
And the gentle sounding flute.

S. S. GREATHEED — THE GARDEN OF JESUS.

In green old gardens, hidden away
From sight of revel and sound of strife . . .
Here may I live what life I please
Married and buried out of sight.

VIOLET FARRE — IN GREEN OLD GARDENS

One should cultivate letters or his garden.

VOLTAIRE — LETTERS

SOME EXCELLENT EXAMPLES OF TOPIARY ARE THESE TWO
YEW TREES, TRIMMED TO THE SHAPES OF A BIRD AND A BEE AT
HEVER CASTLE, KENT

A SET OF SCULPTED CHESS MEN AT HEVER CASTLE

———◇———

'That is well said', replied Candide, 'but we must cultivate our garden'.

VOLTAIRE — CANDIDE

———◇———

So twice five miles of fertile ground
With walls and towers were girdled round:
And there were gardens bright with sinuous rills,
Where blossomed many an incense-bearing tree;
And here were forests ancient as the hills,
Enfolding sunny spots of greenery.

SAMUEL TAYLOR COLERIDGE — KUBLA KHAN

———◇———

Yes, in the poor man's garden grow
Far more than herbs and flowers —
Kind thoughts, contentment, peace of mind,
And joy for weary hours.

MARY HOWITT — THE POOR MAN'S GARDEN

———◇———

I would be back in my own garden
Watching my windy daffodils.

ALINE KILMER — A GUEST SPEAKS

———◇———

One of the greatest gifts of a perfect garden is the gift of solitude, and that is generally beyond the power of the little cottage plot to offer; but, as a source of infinite pleasure to its owner, as a source of pleasure to all who pass by, as a cheering feature of English landscape, and as a great force tending towards contentment and peace, the cottage garden is beyond all praise.

HARRY ROBERTS — *ENGLISH GARDENS*

It is impossible for the most blasé townsman to walk through one of those beautiful villages distributed throughout the south-west of England without being moved by the little gardens that front the cottages on either side of the road. What is it that is so moving? We are not moved in this way by the flower-beds round the Albert Memorial. Yet there can be no doubt that the latter represent an altogether more definite conscious artistic purpose. Does not one of the great differences lie in this: That in the cottage garden the individuality and character and peculiar beauty of each plant is respected; whereas in the more formal and 'artistic' garden the colours and forms of the individual plants are considered as almost nothing in themselves, but only as contributing to some striking mass effect? The typical amateur gardener in this country grows to love his plants almost in the same way as that in which a man is said to love his dog.

HARRY ROBERTS — *ENGLISH GARDENS*

It would never occur to most gardeners to write a poem or paint a picture. Most gardens are the only artistic effort their owners ever make.

HUGH JOHNSON

There is scarcely a cottage in most of the southern parts of England but hath its proportionable garden; so great delight do most men take in it.

WORLIDGE 1680

My delight and thy delight
Walking, like two angels white
In the gardens of the night.

ROBERT BRIDGES

AN
ACCOUNT
OF A
COTTAGE AND GARDEN
NEAR TADCASTER.
WITH
OBSERVATIONS
UPON LABOURERS HAVING FREEHOLD COTTAGES
AND GARDENS,
AND UPON A PLAN FOR SUPPLYING COTTAGERS
WITH COWS.
PRINTED AT THE DESIRE OF THE SOCIETY
FOR BETTERING THE CONDITION, AND
INCREASING THE COMFORTS OF THE POOR

LONDON:
PRINTED FOR T. BECKET, BOOKSELLER, PALL-MALL
1797.
PRICE ONE SHILLING A DOZEN.
'The great specific of the age for the sorrows of the poor was charity'

TITLE PAGE OF 'AN ACCOUNT OF A COTTAGE AND GARDEN' 1797.

*A*nd even in these our daies, under the name of Gardens and Hortyards, there
goe many daintie places of pleasure within the very citie; and under the colour
also and title of them men are possessed of faire closes and pleasant fields, yea,
and of proper houses with a good circuit of ground lying to them, like pretie
fermes and graunges in the countrey; all of which they tearme by the name of
Gardens.

PLINY THE ELDER

A small, convenient and healthy house, a large and well situated garden, a
good library gradually accumulated, a small competency — and what more in
the way of physical possessions can the contemplative man require?

HARRY ROBERTS — ENGLISH GARDENS

*F*air Quiet, have I found thee here,
And Innocence, thy sister dear?

ANDREW MARVELL — THE GARDEN

THE TYPICAL ONE-WHEELED MEDIEVAL WHEELBARROW.

A Source of Infinite Pleasure

THE ITALIAN WALK AT DRAYTON GREEN C. 1838.

*I've often wished that I had clear
For life six hundred pounds a year;
A handsome house to lodge a friend
A river at my garden's end,
A terrace walk, and half a rood
of land set out to plant a wood.*

POPE — IMITATIONS OF HORACE

*This used to be among my prayers — a piece of land not so very large, which
would contain a garden, and near the house a spring of everflowing water, and
beyond these a bit of wood.*

HORACE — SATIRES 30BC

83

LOVE
AND
GARDENS

◇

Down by the salley gardens my love and I did meet;
She passed the salley gardens with little snow white feet,
She bid me take love easy, as the leaves grow on the tree;
But I, being young and foolish, with her would not agree.

In a field by the river my love and I did stand,
And on my leaning shoulder she laid her snow white hand,
She bid me take life easy, as the grass grows on the weirs;
But I was young and foolish, and now am full of tears.

W. B. YEATS

◇

Awake O north wind; and come, thou south, blow upon my garden, that the
spices thereof may flow out. Let my beloved come into his garden and eat his
pleasant fruits.

SONG OF SOLOMON

◇

———◇———

*T*is down in yonder garden green
Love, where we used to walk,
The finest flower that e'er was seen
Is withered to a stalk.

The stalk is withered dry, my love,
So will our hearts decay;
So make yourself content my love
Till God calls you away.

W B YEATS — WALY, WALY (A BALLAD)

———◇———

———◇———

KNOT FROM 'THE COMPLEAT GARDENERS PRACTICE' 1664.

———◇———

There is a garden in her face
Where roses and white lilies grow;
A heav'nly paradise is that place,
Wherein all pleasant fruits do flow.
There cherries grow, which none may buy
Till 'cherry ripe' themselves do cry.

THOMAS CAMPION 1620

Clerk Saunders and May Margaret
Walk'd owre you garden green;
And deep and heavy was the love
That fell thir twa between.

CLERK SAUNDERS — (BALLAD)

RUSTIC ARCH AND CUPID AT DRAYTON GREEN.

William Hooker's figure of William's Bon Chretien Pear 1816.

The timid maid
Pleas'd to be praised and yet of praise affraid
Seeks her best flowers, not those of woods or fields
But such as every farmer's garden yield.
Fine cabbage roses painted like her face
And shining pansys trimmed in golden lace
And tall tuft larkheels featherd thick wi' flowers
And woodbines climbing o'er the door in bowers.
And London tufts of many a mottled hue
And pale pink pea and monkshood darkly blue.
And white and purple jiliflowers that stay
Lingering in blossom summer half away
And single blood walls of a lucious smell
Old fashioned flowers which huswives love so well.
And columbines stone blue or deep night brown
Their honeycomb-like blossoms hanging down.
Each cottage garden's fond adopted child
The heaths still claim them where they yet grow wild,
Mong their old wild companions summer blooms
Furze brake and mozzling ling and golden broom,
Snap dragons gaping like to sleeping clowns
And 'clipping pinks' (which maidens Sunday gowns
Full often wear catcht at by tozing chaps)
Pink as the ribbons round their snowy caps.
'Bess in her bravery' too of glowing dyes
As deep as sunset's crimson-pillow'd skyes
And marjoram notts sweet briar and ribbon grass,
And lavender the choice of every lass
And sprigs of lads love all familiar names
Which every garden thro the village claims.

These the maids gather wi' a coy delight
And tyes them up in readiness for night,
Giving to every swain tween love and shame
Her 'clipping poseys' as their yearly claim,
And turning as he claims the custom kiss
Wi' stifled smiles . . .

JOHN CLARE — THE SHEPHERDS CALENDAR 1824

THE FRONTISPIECE OF 'THE PRACTICAL HUSBANDMAN AND GARDENER'
1733, EDITED BY STEPHEN SWITZER.

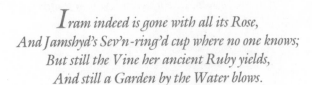

I ram indeed is gone with all its Rose,
And Jamshyd's Sev'n-ring'd cup where no one knows;
But still the Vine her ancient Ruby yields,
And still a Garden by the Water blows.

But still a ruby kindles in the Vine
And many a Garden by the Water blows.

THE RUBAIYAT OF OMAR KHAYYAM

I sometimes think that never blows so red
The rose as where some buried Caesar bled;
That every Hyacinth the Garden wears
Dropt in her Lap from some once lovely Head.

Ah Moon of my Delight who know'st no wane
The Moon of Heav'n is rising once again:
How oft hereafter rising shall she look
Through this same Garden after me — in vain!

You rising Moon that looks for us again.
How oft hereafter will she wax and wane
How oft hereafter rising look for us
Through this same Garden — and for one in vain!

THE RUBAIYAT OF OMAR KHAYYAM

COLOUR
IN THE
GARDEN

◇

This has been described as 'the most beautiful garden at Sissinghurst, and indeed of all England'. It lies at the foot of the Priest's House, and is divided by neat low hedges of box. All the flowers in this garden are white or grey. Lacy white festoons of strong growing roses arch over the centre. Later in the year, generous plantings of Lilium Regale come up through grey artemisia and silvery cineraria maritima. Still later, the great metallic-looking onorpordons grow up, and clouds of gypsophila throw a veil round the pencils of a white Veronica Virginica alba, and a few belated white delphiniums and white eremuri persist. Under the silver willow-leaved pear (Pyrus salicifolia pendula) is a lead statue of a virgin by the Yugoslav sculptor, Rosandic, cast from the walnut original in the library; and on the far side an archway overlooks the rich farmlands of the Weald.

NIGEL NICOLSON DESCRIBING THE WHITE GARDEN AT SISSINGHURST

◇

We find flower-beds habitually considered too much as masses of colour, instead of an assemblage of living beings . . . Gardeners are teaching us to think too little about the plants individually, and to look at them chiefly as an assemblage of beautiful colours. It is difficult in these blooming masses to separate one from another, all produce so much the same sort of impression. The consequence is that people see the flowers in the beds without caring to know anything about them, or even to ask their names.

FORBES-WATSON 1872 — FLOWERS AND GARDENS

◇

◇

The planting of the border is designed to show a distinct scheme of colour arrangement. At the two ends there is a ground work of grey and glaucous foliage Stachys, Santolina, Cineraria Maritima, Sea Kale and Lyme Grass, with darker foliage, also of grey quality, of Yucca, Clematis recta and Rue. With this, at the near or western end, there are flowers of pure blue, grey-blue, white, palest yellow and palest pink, each colour partly in distinct masses and partly intergrouped. The colouring then passes through stronger yellows to orange and red. By the time the middle space of the border is reached the colour is strong and gorgeous, but, as it is in good harmonies, it is never garish. Then the colour strength recedes in an inverse sequence through orange and deep yellow to pale yellow, white and palest pink, with the blue-grey foliage. But at this, the eastern end, instead of the pure blues we have purples and lilacs.

Looked at from a little way forward, for a wide space of grass allows this point of view, the whole border can be seen as one picture, the cool colouring at the ends enhancing the brilliant warmth of the middle. Then passing along the wide path next to the border the value of the colour arrangement is still more strongly felt. Each portion now becomes a picture in itself, and every one is of such a colouring that it best prepares the eye, in accordance with natural law, for what is to follow. Standing for a few moments before the end-most region of grey and blue, and saturating the eye to its utmost capacity with these colours, it passes with extraordinary avidity to the succeeding yellows.

Now the eye has again become saturated, this time with the rich colouring, and has therefore, by the law of complementary colour, acquired a strong appetite for the greys and purples. These therefore assume an appearance of brilliancy that they would not have had without the preparation provided by their recently received complementary colour.

GERTRUDE JEKYLL — COLOUR IN THE FLOWER GARDEN

◇

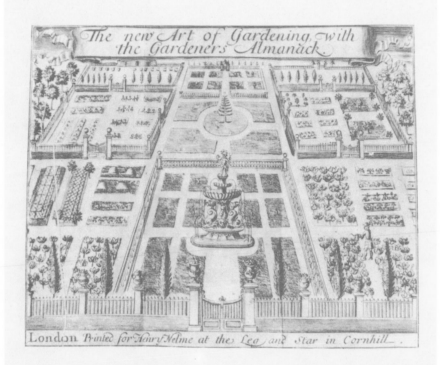

Pictorial plan of a garden from 'The New Art of Gardening'.

A DUTCH GARDEN FROM 'A GARDEN OF FLOWERS' 1615.

STEPPING STONES IN THE GARDEN OF A ZEN TEMPLE IN JAPAN

A GIANT WATER GUM IN SPRING FOLIAGE AT THE BOTANIC GARDENS IN
SYDNEY, AUSTRALIA.

True garden picture-makers are rare indeed. Most of us have to be content with the inherent pleasure in cheerful colours pleasantly organized avoiding, as far as we can, the 'riot' threatened on so many seed packets.

Up to a point the season dictates the rules. Winter reduces the palette but finds a lovely equilibrium in its muted range of browns, greys and purples. Spring juggles with contrasts of the most daring kind. Summer provokes us with its heavy green mantle to set out our most flaunting colours. Autumn strikes great chords of harmony with its turning leaves, dominating whatever we do.

The gardener's thoughts on colour are bound to be seasonal. They will grow in coherence and authority if they follow certain rules experience has shown to be widely applicable. The first is that colour-contrasts in themselves quickly become wearisome: especially if the colours are in anything like equal quantities. It is no new discovery that red stands out in sharp relief against green, or that grey and purple foliage are powerful foils for each other. There may well be a place for both these contrasts in your garden, but only as an isolated and climactic moment. It is almost always a mistake to make contrast a theme . . .

Any contrast should be heavily weighted on one side or the other, with one colour unmistakably dominant. Where the contrast involved a strong colour and a weaker one, it is the weaker one that should predominate in area. Small areas of light colours among large ones of stronger tones seem feeble and indecisive, whereas one strong colour dotted here and there on a quiet ground can be very effective.

HUGH JOHNSON — THE PRINCIPLES OF GARDENING

GARDEN LORE

---◇---

The soil is rather like a bran-tub — you only get out of it what you put in.

RHS ENCYCLOPEDIA OF GARDENING

---◇---

Doves dung is ye best, because the same possesseth a mighty hoteness. The dung also of the hen and other foules greatly commended for the sournesse, except ye dung of geese ducks and other waterfoules.

A commendation next is attributed to the Asses dung, in that the same beast for his leisurely eating, digesteth easier, and causeth the better dung.

The third place is the Goates dung, after this both ye Oxe and Cow dung; next the Swines dung, worthier than the Oxen or Kine. The vilest and worst of all dungs after the opinion of the Greek writers of Husbandry, is the horse and moiles.

The dung which men make (if the same be not mixed with the rabbith, or dust swept out of the house) is greatly mislyked, for that by nature it is hoter, and burneth the seedes sowne in that earth: so that this is not to be used, unlesse the grounde be a barren, gravelly or verie loose sand, lacking strength in it.

The mud also of running water, as the ditch or river, may bee employed instead of dung.

If no kind of dung can be purchased, then in gravelly grounds it shall be best to dung the same with Chalke.

FROM THE GARDENER'S LABYRINTH

———◇———

Sow carrots in your Gardens, and humbly praise God for them, as for a singular and great blessing.

PROFITABLE INSTRUCTIONS FOR . . . KITCHEN GARDENS 1599

———◇———

. . . The toad, without which no garden would be complete.

CHARLES DUDLEY WARNER

———◇———

———◇———

MEDIEVAL GARDENERS.
NOTE THE CLUMSY WOODEN SPADES.

———◇———

Companionable Plants

Roses are susceptible to attacks from aphids, caterpillars, beetles of several kinds and spiders. They can be protected to a certain extent by companions. Parsley repels rose beetles, and there are several plants of the *allium* family — garlic, shallots, onions and the ornamental onions grown for their attractive flowers — that will give roses considerable protection from all aphids.

If there is room in the rose-bed one or two tomato plants will be most beneficial as they discourage black-spot. Tomatoes, however would look out of place in a rose-bed, but it has been suggested that a spray can be made from tomato leaves. Put a few handfuls of tomato leaves in an electric liquidiser, add the pulp to 3 litres of mild soapy water, strain, and spray in the usual way.

Poisonous plants

Monkshood	all parts
Pasque flower	young plants & flowers
Box	leaves
Clematis	leaves
Autumn Crocus	leaves
Lily of the Valley	leaves & flowers
Daphne	leaves, bark & berries
Larkspur Delphinium	young plants & seeds
Foxglove	leaves
Euphorbias	milky sap
Poinsettia	leaves
Ivy	leaves & berries
Hellebores	leaves
Hydrangea	leaves
Hypericum	all parts when eaten
Busy Lizzie	young stems & leaves

Laburnum	leaves & seeds
Laurel	all parts
Privet	leaves & berries
Lobelia	leaves, stems
Lupinus	leaves, pods, seeds
Oleander	all parts
Star of Bethlehem	all parts
Poppy	unripe seed pod
Mistletoe	berries
Pittosporum	leaves & stems, fruit
Primrose	leaves & stems
Cherries, peaches & plums	seeds & leaves
Buttercup	leaves
Rhubarb	leaves
Rhododendron & Azalea	leaves & all parts
Elderberry	shoots, leaves, bark
Tansy	leaves
Wisteria, Yew	foliage , bark, seeds

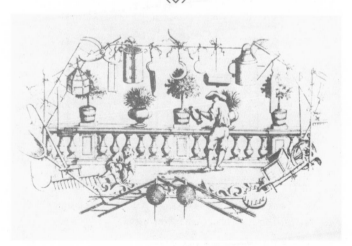

In The Garden

JANUARY • Pray for snow to make digging impossible
FEBRUARY • Eradicate weeds from lawn
MARCH • Sow new lawn
APRIL • Clear paths and drive with flame gun
MAY • Replace edging plants of paths and drive
JUNE • Make up cat's bed under cloches
JULY • Plant out winter supply of broccoli, brussel sprouts for pigeons
AUGUST • Water if dry. Don't water if wet
SEPTEMBER • Try to prevent wife ordering more roses
OCTOBER • Prepare new bed for more roses
NOVEMBER • Settle down for winter study of catalogues
DECEMBER • Continue winter study of catalogues and keep all pips from
Christmas oranges, tangerines, date and avocado stones, etc. Pot up and put on
kitchen window sill.

SPIKE HUGHES — THE COARSE GARDENER'S CALENDAR 1968

MEDIEVAL GARDENERS USING A RAKE, ONE TOOL WHICH HAS CHANGED
LITTLE OVER THE CENTURIES.

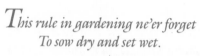

This rule in gardening ne'er forget
To sow dry and set wet.

JOHN RAY — ENGLISH PROVERBS

I value my garden more for being full of blackbirds than of cherries, and very
frankly give them fruit for their songs.

ADDISON 1672-1719

Who loves a garden loves a greenhouse too.

COWPER — THE TASK

The owners of Hives have a perfite forsight and knowledge what the increase or
yeelde of honye will be everie yeare, by the plentiful or small number of floures
growing and appearing on the Tyme about the Sommer solstice. For this
increaseth and yeeldeth most friendly floures for the Bees which render a coloure
and savoure to the Hony.

THOMAS HYLL — THE PROFITABLE ART OF GARDENING 1568

Broome and the strawberrie-tree are not altogether good for to make hony and
boxe maketh honie of a bad smell and which troubleth their braines that eat it.

FROM MAISON RUSTIQUE OR THE COUNTRY FARME

But how dull and silent the place would be without the beehives. The gardener does not 'hold with them foreign bees,' and his strain are the good old English black bee, the best tempered, the most hard working and the most lovable bees in the world. Their hives, placed where the first rays of light will fall on them, are painted blue, for that, he says, is the colour they love most. The custom is still maintained of telling them just anything that betides any member of the house, and perhaps that is why they are such friendly bees and give such good honey. To listen to this bee-master is entrancing, and one cannot help thinking that there is more in lore, handed down through the ages, than we in our ignorance can understand. Perhaps it is true that there is no honey so good as that taken from a hive immediately after a rainbow, and why should not the magic of the stars — those glorious flowers in the garden of space — overrule the bees?

ELEANOUR SINCLAIR ROHDE — THE OLD ENGLISH GARDENING BOOKS

PORTRIT OF THOMAS HYLL, FROM 'A PLEASANT INSTRUCTION OF THE PARFIT ORDERINGE OF BEES' 1568.

A place open to the South sun and yet notwithstanding neither exceeding in heat nor in cold, defended from windes and tempests, so that they may flie their sundrie and several waies to get diversitie of pastures, and so againe may returne to their little cottages laden with their composition of honey: and again in such a place as wherein there is great quantity of thyme, orgaine, savorie . . .

The place must be closed with a very strong hedge or else with good wals, for feare both of beasts and theeves: for kine and sheep do eat up their flowres, and beate the dew off from the flowres.

. . . serpents also doe sometimes take up their Innes in their hives, but to take away this Casualtie at once and for ever. You must plant rue round about them in good quantitie, in as much as venemous beastes cannot abide this herbe . . .

But whatever the place is, whether in the garden of pleasure or elsewhere . . . it must not be hemde in with high wals on every side; and yet if for feare of theeves you were disposed to raise them the higher, then you must pearse the wall some three feete from the ground, and worke it with small holes, for the bees to flie through at, and some twentie or thirtie paces off to build some little house. if you be so disposed, for him to dwell in who hath the charge of looking to them, and therein also to put his tooles.

CHARLES STEVENS AND JOHN LIEBAULT — MAISON RUSTIQUE 1600.

THE POLLARD VISTA SEEN FROM THE LAWN AT DRAYTON GREEN.

Tools

The earliest books on gardening have little to say about tools, but something may be gathered from medieval carvings and illustrations in old manuscripts. In Lincoln Cathedral there is a misericord with a carving of an old gardener carrying an iron shod spade and primitive drawings of Adam and Eve, and Cain and Abel show them with spades, axes and a tool resembling the narrow hoe used by gardeners today.

John Rea, who in 1662 published his 'Flora, Ceres and Pomona' is more explicit. He says that the garden should have a tool house, with 'a fine wire riddle, two spades — a bigger and a lesser — likewise shovels, hoes of several sizes, a pruning hook, grafting knives, a saw, chisel, mallet, a small pen-knife for innoculating and layering gillyflowers, a line and rule, trowels of several sizes, two iron rakes — one long and bigger in the head, the other smaller, with teeth thicker set — and several baskets of twigs and besoms to sweep the garden.'

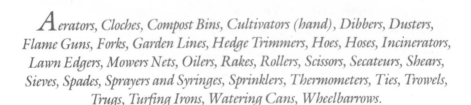

Aerators, Cloches, Compost Bins, Cultivators (hand), Dibbers, Dusters, Flame Guns, Forks, Garden Lines, Hedge Trimmers, Hoes, Hoses, Incinerators, Lawn Edgers, Mowers Nets, Oilers, Rakes, Rollers, Scissors, Secateurs, Shears, Sieves, Spades, Sprayers and Syringes, Sprinklers, Thermometers, Ties, Trowels, Trugs, Turfing Irons, Watering Cans, Wheelbarrows.

TOOLS AND EQUIPMENT LISTED IN *READER'S DIGEST GARDENING YEAR.*

What a man needs in gardening is a cast iron back, with a hinge in it.

CHARLES DUDLEY WARNER 1829-1900

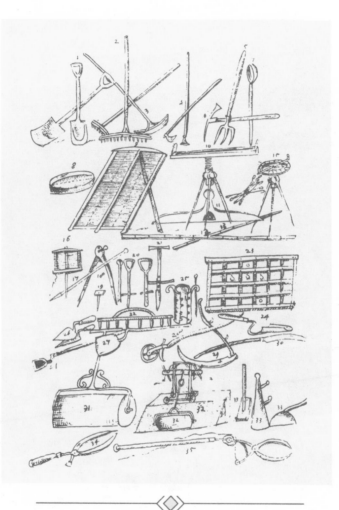

JOHN EVELYN'S SKETCHES FOR 'ELYSIUM BRITTANNICUM' A BOOK HE
NEVER COMPLETED. DRAWN BEFORE 1659, THEY SHOW AN AMAZING
RANGE OF TOOLS.

The market is the best garden.
GEORGE HERBERT — JACULA PRUDENTUM

A GARDENER'S TOOLSHED OF 1706, INCLUDING, ON THE WALL, SOME
SURVEYING IMPLEMENTS.

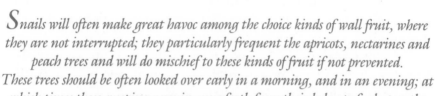

Snails will often make great havoc among the choice kinds of wall fruit, where they are not interrupted; they particularly frequent the apricots, nectarines and peach trees and will do mischief to these kinds of fruit if not prevented.

These trees should be often looked over early in a morning, and in an evening; at which times these creeping vermin come forth from their holes, to feed upon the fruit, and may then be readily taken and destroyed.

. . . As soon as insects appear upon any part of the (fruit) trees, endeavour as much as possible to destroy them; and the only method is this:

First, pull off all the worst leaves that are infested with them; that is, such as are shrivelled, or much curled up; then strew some tobacco dust over all the branches and leaves; let this remain on the trees two or three days; then you may wash it off, by giving the trees a hearty watering all over their branches; but if it is suffered to remain, it will do the trees no harm.

Let the trees after this, be frequently watered, in dry weeather, all over their branches; for this will do a great deal in destroying and preventing the insects from breeding.

For the purpose of watering the branches of wall-trees, there is nothing so useful and convenient as a small hand engine . . . These engines are both handy and cheap. The best are those made of tin, and may be bought at any of the tin-shops for about six or eight shillings according to the size.

THOMAS MAWE (GARDENER TO HIS GRACE THE DUKE OF LEEDS) — EVERY MAN HIS OWN
GARDENER 1767

There are fairies at the bottom of our garden.
ROSE FYLEMAN

Four leaf clover

For centuries they have been believed to be lucky. It was thought in Germany that one could summon up a witch by carrying a four leaf clover on Christmas Eve.

St Patrick taught the doctrine of the trinity by showing people a clover leaf. Even before Christianity the leaves were said to represent the three worlds of nature — sea, earth and heavens.

Pliny tells us that serpents are never found around a clover.

Some Superstitions concerning parsley

Babies are found in parsley beds.

You may steal parsley but never accept it as a gift.

Never transplant parsley in Devonshire, it will offend the faires and ill luck will befall you.

When in love, don't cut parsley.

The Greeks associated parsely with death.

A MEDIEVAL SIEVE, WITH THE MATERIAL TO BE SIEVED THROWN AGAINST THE MESH.

THOMAS MAWSON DESIGNED THIS TERRACE GARDEN IN THE 1890S.

GOD AND GARDENS

God the first garden made, and the first city Cain.

ABRAHAM COWLEY

A garden is a lovesome thing, God wot!
Rose plot, Fringed pool, Ferned grot —
The veriest school
Of peace; and yet the fool
Contends that God is not
Not God! in gardens! when the eve is cool?
Nay, but I have a sign:
'Tis very sure God walks in mine.

T E BROWN — MY GARDEN

A touch divine —
And the scaled eyeball owns the mystic rod;
Visibly through his garden walketh God.

ROBERT BROWNING — SORDELLO

GOD AND GARDENS

My Tent stands in a garden
Of aster and golden-rod,
Tilled by the rain and the sunshine
And sown by the hand of God.

BLISS CARMAN — AN AUTUMN GARDEN

God Almighty first planted a garden. And indeed, it is the purest of human
pleasures.

FRANCIS BACON

AN EARLY ENGRAVING BY J. PINE (1690-1756) OF A PINEAPPLE FLOWERING.

In The Garden

*A*nd the Lord God planted a garden eastward in Eden. The tree of life also in the midst of the garden. And they heard the voice of the Lord God walking in the garden in the cool of the day.

GENESIS

*T*he kiss of the sun for pardon
The song of the birds for mirth,
One is nearer God's heart in a garden
Than anywhere else on earth.

DOROTHY FRANCES GURNEY 1858-1932

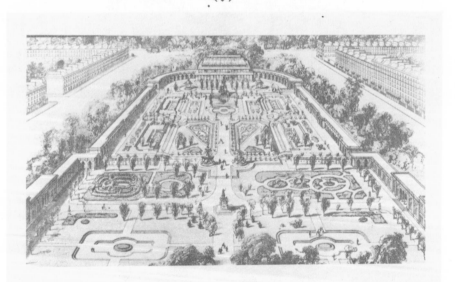

VICTORIAN GEOMETRIC DESIGN CAN BE SEEN IN THE GARDENS OF THE
ROYAL HORTICULTURAL SOCIETY, KENSINGTON 1861.

◇

The best place to seek God is in a garden. You can dig for him there.

GEORGE BERNARD SHAW — BLACK GIRL IN HER SEARCH FOR GOD.

◇

For one night or the other night
Will come the Gardener in white.
And gathered flowers are dead,
Yasmin.

ELROY FLECKER — HASSAN

◇

◇

DECIMUS BURTON'S PALM HOUSE, KEW (1844-8) WAS A VITAL
DEVELOPMENT IN GLASS-HOUSE CONSTRUCTION.

◇

Acknowledgements

The Publishers gratefully acknowledge the contributions of the originators of the works and sayings quoted in the book. Every effort has been made to trace the ownership of copyright in the extracts included in this anthology. Any omission is purely inadvertent and will be corrected in subsequent editions, provided written notification is given to the book's creators: The Watermark Press, 29a King Street, Sydney, NSW 2000.

Page 32 AKENFIELD by Ronald Blyth published by Penguin Books
Page 93 PORTRAIT OF A MARRIAGE by Nigel Nicolson published by Weidenfeld Nicolson
Page 97 PRINCIPLES OF GARDENING by Hugh Johnston published by Mitchell Beazley
Page 102 THE ART OF COARSE GARDENING by Spike Hughes published by Century Hutchinson

PICTURE CREDITS
All colour photographs by Simon Blackall
cover photograph: Moss garden, Kyoto, Japan.